This book belongs to

ARYA RAOL ‼ ‼ ♡

WITH LOTS OF LOVE

‼ *JHANVI BHUA* ‼
&
♡ *JAI BHUA* ♡

Short Stories from
Indian Mythology

Short Stories from
Indian Mythology

ANURAG MEHTA

Nita Mehta
PUBLICATIONS

Short Stories from Indian Mythology

Reprint 2009

ISBN 978-81-7676-074-4

Illustrations: **Nita Mehta** Enriching Young Minds
Artist: Suvidha Mistry

Layout and Laser Typesetting:

National Information Technology Academy
3A/3, Asaf Ali Road
New Delhi-110002
☎ 23252948

Price: Rs. 295/-

Published by:

Nita Mehta
Enriching Young Minds

3A/3 Asaf Ali Road, New Delhi-110002
Tel: 91-11-23250091, 29214011, 23252948, 29218574
Fax: 91-11-29225218, 91-11-23250091
E-Mail   : nitamehta@nitamehta.com
            nitamehta@email.com
Website : http://www.nitamehta.com,
            http://www.snabindia.com

Contributing Writers:
Subhash Mehta
Tanya Mehta

Editorial & Proofreading:
Ekta
Deepali

Printed at:
BATRA ART PRESS, NEW DELHI

Distributed by:
THE VARIETY BOOK DEPOT
A.V.G. Bhavan, M 3 Con Circus
New Delhi - 110 001
Tel: 23417175, 23412567; Fax: 23415335
Email: varietybookdepot@rediffmail.com

Contents

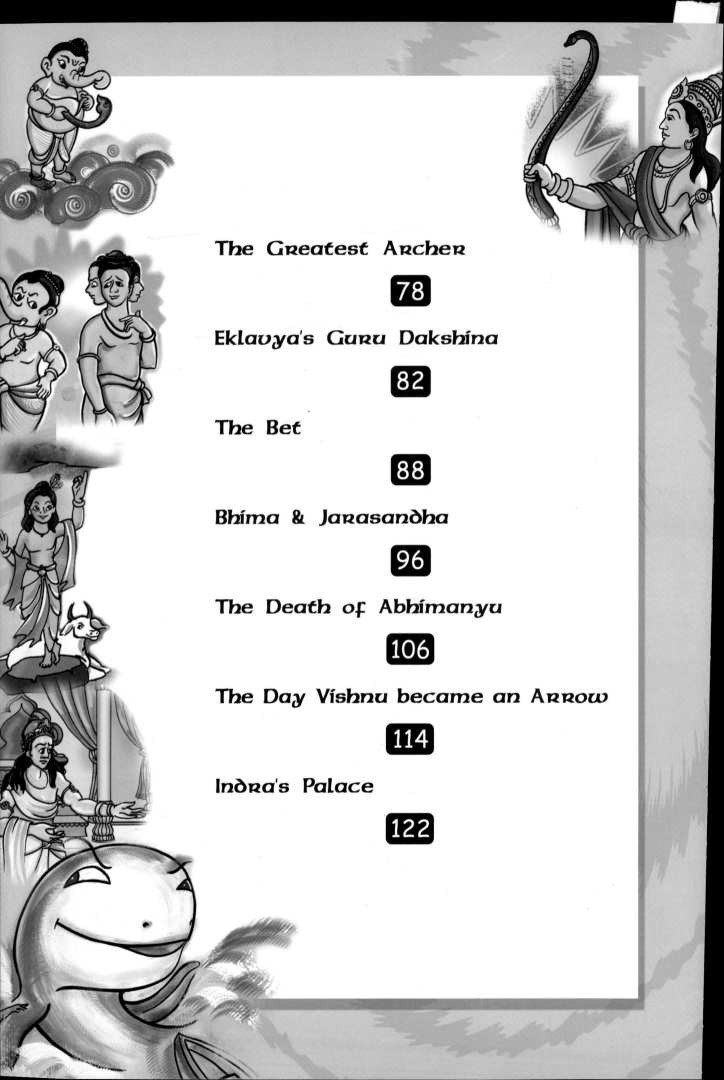

Introduction

Picked from the infinite treasury of legends emerging out of Indian mythology, these short stories represent the diverse formats of adventures, moral messages and the richness of the Indian style of story telling. The narratives are simple and involving, making sure that the readers do not lose their grip on the story line even for one moment. These stories incorporate a reality into the everyday lives of the characters described- may they be gods or humans, reiterating the fact that our universe binds all of us with its rules, firmly stating that even divinity is not spared.

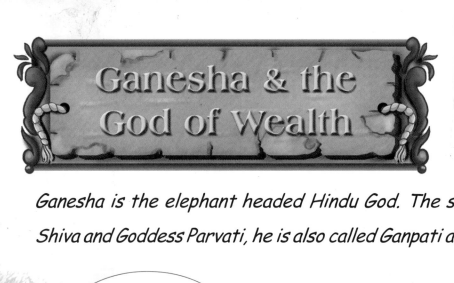

Ganesha & the God of Wealth

Ganesha is the elephant headed Hindu God. The son of Lord Shiva and Goddess Parvati, he is also called Ganpati and Vinayak.

"I really have a lot of riches," bragged Kuber, the treasurer of the heavens, vainly to himself.

"I think I will go to Mount Kailash and invite Lord Shiva and his spouse Goddess Parvati for a meal. They will come to my celestial kingdom of Alkapuri and see for themselves how wealthy I am."

Deciding this, Kuber presented himself in front of Shiva.

"Thank you so much Kuber, for your kind invitation," answered Shiva when Kuber requested him to come for lunch.

"But, I am afraid, I will have to refuse," continued Shiva, "Parvati and I have pressing engagements elsewhere."

Shiva knew quite well why he was being invited. Kuber had always been a silly show-off. Kuber was unable to hide his disappointment, so Shiva quickly added, "I suggest you take Ganesha with you for lunch."

Ganesha nodded his head happily. He loved food and a lunch invitation promised a great deal of good eats.

Kuber, of course, kept boasting about his glory and his own riches as Ganesha accompanied him back to Alkapuri. Finally, Kuber and Ganesha reached Alkapuri.

Soon, Ganesha was greeted with a traditional perfumed bath as part of an extravagant welcome at the palace entrance. After that, they entered into the luxurious palace. Kuber proudly strutted along the ornate corridors, hoping Ganesha was noticing his prosperity.

Ganesha was led to an even more grand dining area. Servants carrying trays, laden with food, lined the hall. Overjoyed, Ganesha sat down to eat. His appetite was ravenous. He finished off all that was served to him.

"Bring me more food. Get me all the cooked food in the kitchen," demanded Ganesha. Hurriedly, the palace servants ran up and down serving Ganesha who seemed to be very hungry. The servants huffed, puffed and panted, piling food into Ganesha's plate. Ganesha ate and ate and ate. Dishes emptied faster than they could be filled.

"I am still hungry," Ganesha said impatiently, "I want more food."

"The food is finished, sire," the head cook whispered to Kuber.

Ganesha heard that and bellowed, "What? The food has finished!

But I am still hungry," Ganesha grabbed his plate and munched it up. The servants as well as Kuber shrank in fear. Ganesha ran to the kitchen and began to eat the empty vessels too! Then, he went to Kuber's treasury and began eating the pearls, gold and gems. Kuber saw his boundless treasure dwindling before his eyes, until all that remained were a couple of pearls in the corner. Kuber could have cried in anguish. His treasury had never looked so empty. Still, Ganesha was not satisfied.

Oh no! Not my treasury

Ganesha went on eating everything that came his way.

Gasp! Even the furniture of the palace, the gardens, the trees, everything! He began to eat through the city of Alkapuri.

Kuber watched horrified. He stood with folded hands and appealed to Ganesha not to destroy his city.

"I am still hungry," said Ganesha. Then, Kuber noticed the little God looking at him with a wicked gleam in his eyes.

"Since there is nothing left to eat," said Ganesha, "I think I'll eat you."

Kuber fled with the little God close behind. He ran to Shiva and fell at his feet, quivering with fear.

"Help! My Almighty Lord, help! Ganesha is eating everything.

His hunger is insatiable. He is threatening to eat me too. Save me," begged Kuber. Shiva smiled and said,

"Kuber, take this roasted rice and feed Ganesha."

Kuber bowed humbly and served Ganesha. Ganesha ate the roasted rice and suddenly he was not hungry any more.

"I am full now," sighed Ganesha.

Kuber heaved a sigh of relief. He saw Ganesha and Shiva smiling at each other and realized he had been guilty of pride and vanity.

"Forgive me, Lord, for my false pride in my wealth. I had forgotten that it is you who gave it to me."

Thus, saying so, Kuber left.

Later, Kuber thought to himself,

"Lord Ganesha taught me a good lesson. By demanding more food, he was showing me that even the best of cuisine brought to him with an intention to show off, brings no satisfaction. Yet, just a handful of ordinary roasted rice, given with love and devotion gave him so much of contentment and he was happy. I was wrong to have expressed my love and devotion to God by material wealth and not by genuine feelings."

The Moon Teases Ganesha

Ganesha has his own vehicle to ride. Do you know what? A rat! Thus, it is said that Ganesha has the extreme strength of an elephant to bulldoze his way on the surface and also the intricate agility of a rat to burrow and manoeuvre under surface.

"Aha, today is my birthday and I shall eat lots of *laddoos*," Ganesha slurped to his rat.

"Let's go! A devotee has invited me to his house for a feast."

Ganesha was extremely happy when he saw the pile of *laddoos* set before him at the devotee's home.

"Munch-yum-munch-munch!" Ganesha eagerly picked off the *laddoos* with his trunk from the plate. He ate and ate till his belly began to swell. "Burp!" went Ganesha and his belly shook!

"Now, I am satisfied! I have eaten so many *laddoos* that I can hardly move! Rat, take me home." He mounted his rat and left.

The rat with Ganesha on his back weaved through paths. Suddenly, a snake abruptly came in their way! The rat skidded and in doing so, he threw Ganesha off!

Bump! Ganesha rolled and with a thump, his stomach burst open!

Plonk-plonk-plonk! *Laddoos* spilled from his tummy. Horrified, Ganesha looked around, his trunk curling with acute embarrassment. He was sure that no one was around to see his ridiculous situation.

"Wait, rat! Let me put the *laddoos* back into my stomach," Ganesha uttered. He quickly filled his stomach again, but realized that the *laddoos* kept spilling out from his open belly.

"Aha! I have an idea," Ganesha muttered, glancing at the slinking snake.

Whup! He seized the snake.

"Sorry snake, I am going to use you as a belt to hold my tummy full of *laddoos*."

Saying so, Ganesha did just that. He tightened the 'snake belt' and held back all the *laddoos* into his big belly.

"Let's go," Ganesha instructed his ride. Just as Ganesha remounted his vehicle, he heard a chuckle.

"Who is that?" Ganesha curiously flapped his ears and looked around. There was no one on the surface.

"Ha-ha-ha, so funny, ha-ha! Using a snake belt to stop *laddoos* from spilling," again someone giggled.

Now, Ganesha was extremely angry. Who was mocking at him? He looked up and saw the culprit. It was the moon. The moon was giggling helplessly at the sight of Ganesha and his stomach full of *laddoos* tied with a snake.

Ganesha went crimson with anger.

"How dare you laugh at me?" shouted Ganesha at the moon. But the moon was quite taken in by the funny sight and kept up his smirk.

This further angered Ganesha and he broke a part of his tusk and hurled it at the moon, saying wrathfully, "I curse you! You will never shine at night now!"

Till then, the moon used to shine every night. But as soon as Ganesha cursed it, the moon disappeared and the sky went inky black. Ganesha rode off fuming.

"Aieeee!!! Where is the moon?" the people on earth frantically asked. "Where is the moon?" inquired the Gods in heaven too!

Nights became miserable for the earth and heaven residents. Gloomy darkness besieged them every evening.

"This is Ganesha's doing. He is angry with the moon for laughing at him. Let's go and beg Ganesha to forgive the moon," suggested someone.

So people, accompanied by the Gods, went to Ganesha and pleaded,

"Please bring the moon back. Please forgive it for laughing at you."

Now, Ganesha was not someone who carried grudges.

"Hmmm, I will bring the moon back," said Ganesha. Everyone clapped happily at this.

"But, on one condition," declared Ganesha, still a little miffed at the moon's audacity.

"What condition?" queried all.

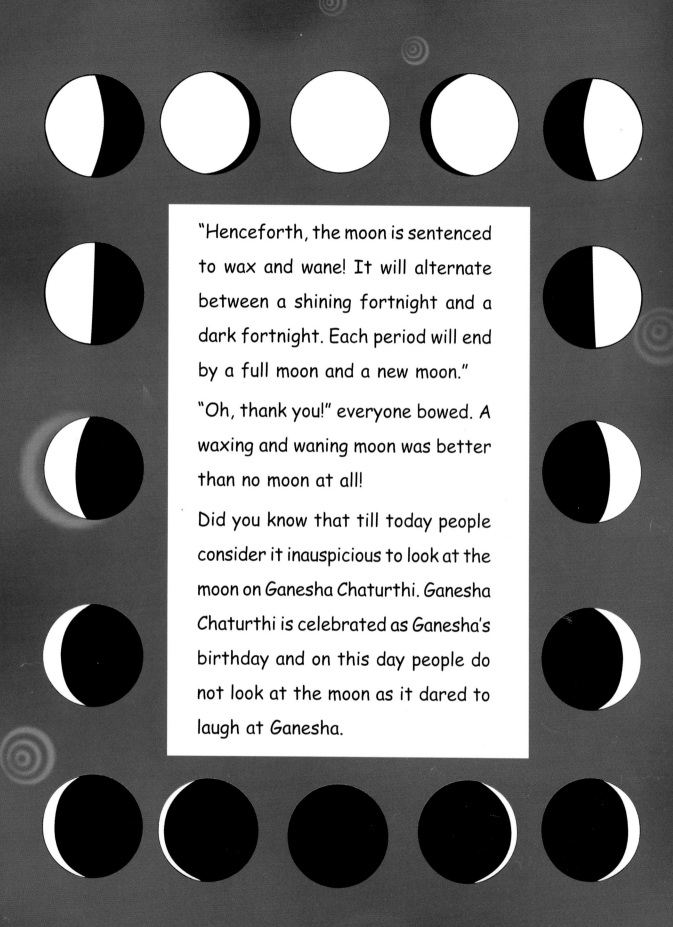

"Henceforth, the moon is sentenced to wax and wane! It will alternate between a shining fortnight and a dark fortnight. Each period will end by a full moon and a new moon."

"Oh, thank you!" everyone bowed. A waxing and waning moon was better than no moon at all!

Did you know that till today people consider it inauspicious to look at the moon on Ganesha Chaturthi. Ganesha Chaturthi is celebrated as Ganesha's birthday and on this day people do not look at the moon as it dared to laugh at Ganesha.

Hanuman & the Sun

Hanuman is the Hindu Monkey God. He is the son of the God of Wind, Vayu and a celestial fairy Anjana. Anjana was cursed to live on earth as a monkey woman and gave birth to Hanuman who is known by many other names; Bajrangbali, Chiranjivi and Pavanputra.

One bright sunny day, Anjana went for a walk along with young Hanuman.

"Mother, look," said little Hanuman as he pointed his tiny fingers towards the sun. Anjana smiled indulgently and looked up too.

"Mother!" Hanuman lisped, "What is that round, shining thing?"

"That is the sun," answered his mother. Hanuman gazed up. His small face shifted from side to side, in curiosity. Little Hanuman thought that the intense brightness of the round, blazing object, needed to be inspected.

With an agile spring, Hanuman reached out and tried to grab the sun. Seeing this, the sun jumped and warned, "Hey, stay away, whaaa!"

But Hanuman had grasped the sun firmly in his hands.

"Ow! Let go, let go, yeow! What is the meaning of this?" the sun bawled helplessly.

Hanuman inquisitively rolled the sun around his fingers. The sun's face cringed and cawed at this intrusion. But Hanuman was not letting go. Looking at the sun, he chuckled,

"This is a ball, mother."

Before Anjana could stop him, Hanuman began to dribble the sun like a ball. The sun groaned and winced in pain.

"Uhhhhhhh-ouch-ow akkkk!! Help! Somebody help me," shuddered the bouncing sun.

"Oh, this is so much fun," Hanuman gurgled, ignoring the sun's discomfort.

"Lord Indra, keeper of the sky, save me from this monkey boy," shrieked the wreathing sun.

Whoooosh! The sky thundered in response to an arrival. Yes, the arrival was that of the Sky God, Indra, who rode his elephant, Airawat.

Hanuman ignored the God of thunder and lightening and continued to play with his sun ball. A little miffed that his arrival did not have the desired impact, Indra clapped louder than usual and said,

"Stop dribbling the sun at once!"

Hanuman was having such an enjoyable time that he refused to listen. If Indra ran this side, Hanuman dribbled to the other side. Indra huffed and puffed across the skies trying to stop Hanuman.

"Who is this impertinent monkey boy who flies like the wind and defies me, the mighty keeper of the skies?" boiled Indra as he chased Hanuman. But there was no catching the son of Vayu.

Indra got so frustrated that his anger spilled over into dark sinister clouds. Angry growls rumbled across the heavens.

Holding the reins of his elephant, Indra thundered,

"Put the sun back."

But Hanuman was not listening! By now, Indra was so enraged that he was not thinking straight. He wanted to get even with this teasing monkey boy. Indra reached out to his quiver full of thunderbolts and picked one.

"Hark! I am throwing this *Vajra* (divine weapon) at you. Beware of its effects," he bellowed dramatically.

Indra threw the bolt with one strong swift blow towards
Hanuman. The weapon struck its target.

Little Hanuman fell down unconscious. Anjana was horrified. She
cried out Hanuman's name desperately, trying to revive him. The sun
vaulted back to its place and Indra left, having completed his task of
saving the sun. Somewhere else, an inner instinct, that his son needed him,
disturbed Lord Vayu. With a rush of airstream, he curved towards the
valley of flowers.

"Hanuman! What happened?" cried Lord Vayu. Anjana continued sobbing
not answering Vayu. "Open your eyes! Wake up Hanuman!"

Vayu wailed, shaking his unconscious son. But Hanuman's innocent face was still. He did not open his eyes. Lord Vayu blustered a current of air, bawling, "Tell me who did this to little Hanuman?"

Getting no answers, the angry Vayu swooped up his son and revolved around outer space. "I am taking the air from the three worlds with me. Air will only come back when Hanuman breathes again."

This was really bad news. All of us know we breathe air to live. Vayu taking away all the air from the world left the plants, animals and people gasping for breath.

"Forgive us. Give us air or else we will die," they choked at Vayu to relent from his curse. But Lord Vayu was so infuriated that he refused to budge. As there was no air, all living things began to wither. Indra was passing over the world and was startled to see what had happened. When he realized that this was all his doing, he was filled with repentance.

"What have I done? That was Lord Vayu's son. Oh! My anger has caused this mess," Lord Indra reproached himself.

"I shall apologize to Lord Vayu," decided Indra.

Lord Indra along with the other Gods approached Lord Vayu. Respectfully, they apologized to him.

Furthermore, with the divine powers vested in them, they revived Hanuman. In addition, they blessed Hanuman with untold powers and immortality. They declared, "None will ever equal you in strength and speed." This made Lord Vayu very happy and he restored air back to the world. Thus, the world was saved and everything came back to normal.

The Breaking of the Bow

In the state of Mithila, the saintly King Janak, had four daughters of marriageable age. The most beautiful amongst them was Sita and many princes desired her as their bride. Janak announced,

"Sita will marry the bravest and the strongest prince in the country." The king had an unstrung bow of Lord Shiva's which was very strong and heavy.

He said, "The prince who can string this bow and break it, will win Sita."

Now, the bow of Lord Shiva could actually not be broken by mortals. Only a God could handle it. Sita had surprised the court by lifting the bow easily, as a child. Unknown to most, Sita was the incarnation of Goddess Lakshmi.

King Janak had found her as a baby, in the furrows of a field and adopted her as his daughter. The people of the kingdom considered her blessed.

Vishwamitra was aware of Sita's true being and knowing that she and Ram were destined to wed on earth, had led the young prince to Mithila. Ram was the incarnation of Lord Vishnu, who was born as the son of King Dashrath of Ayodhya.

At a ceremony called the *Swayamvara*, Janak ordered his men to fetch the bow from its iron box, kept upon an eight-wheeled chariot. It was placed in the middle of a large hall, filled with many nobles. One after the other, various princes tried to lift the bow of Shiva. None, including the most powerful demon king, Ravan, could move it. It created terror amongst cowards and for the selfish, it was unapproachable.

Now it was Ram's turn to lift the bow. Respectfully, he saluted it and prayed for strength. Then, without any effort, he lifted the bow, placed one end against his toe and bent the bow to string it. Everyone was stunned to see the bow snap in two.

The court was filled with shouts of, "Victory to Ram! Glory to Ram."

Sita was delighted. She had seen Ram enter and had hoped that he would become her bridegroom. King Janak sent a messenger to Ayodhya informing them about Ram winning the hand of Sita in marriage. Dashrath gladly gave his consent and came to Mithila with the royal family and courtiers. Janak arranged a grand wedding.

The ceremony had just begun when *Parshuram*, a warrior who protected *rishis* against tyrannical kings, arrived in a terrible rage.

He had learnt about Vishwamitra's training of Ram and the breaking of Shiva's Bow.

Wielding his axe, he threatened Ram, "How dare you break the bow that belonged to Shiva? I will kill you for it." Ram tried to reason with him, but Parshuram insisted on attacking him. Left with no choice, Ram accepted the challenge with great courage.

Seeing Ram's modesty and heroism, Parshuram realized that Ram was indeed the incarnation of Lord Vishnu.

Parshuram acknowledged his mistake and departed in shame.

Janak then led Sita to Ram and placing her hand in his, said, "O Ram, from now onwards, Sita is your life partner. She will follow you as your shadow."

Sita put a garland around Ram's neck and Ram and Sita were wedded. Along with them, Ram's three brothers married Sita's three sisters. A joyous marriage procession reached Ayodhya with magnificently decorated chariots, horses, elephants and bullock carts. The kingdom celebrated the happy event with much pomp and gaiety.

The Race

One day, voices resounded in and out of the environs of Mount Kailash. The two brothers, Ganesha and Kartekeya were arguing.

"Brother, believe me! I am older than you," Ganesha stated as a matter of fact.

"No!" contradicted his brother Kartekeya, "I am the elder between the two of us."

Why were the two brothers quarrelling? Actually, it all started when the Gods of heaven presented Shiva and Parvati with a rare fruit. Now the brothers verbally tangled over who should get the fruit.

"The elder one should," mused their parents. Sigh! And that's how a strife between the brothers ensued. Soon, the dispute heated up and finally their parents had to intervene. "Father, tell him that I am the elder of the two! I should get the fruit," blurted Ganesha, his trunk curling and whirling agitatedly.

Here I go

Kartekeya shrugged saying, "Father, Mother! Convince Ganesha that I am elder!"

"This is getting quite serious," Shiva whispered to his wife.

"Yes! The brothers are getting into a terrible quarrel, sire. Do something," Parvati urged.

"Very well," Shiva pondered and then spoke,

"Sons, we will resolve your argument with a solution. Whoever can tour the whole world and come back first to this starting point, will be given the right to be the elder brother and get the fruit."

"Here I go," declared Kartekeya. Before anything, he flew off at once on his vehicle, the peacock, to make a circuit of the world.

But Ganesha did not move. His vehicle, the rat, was raring to go, but Ganesha just sat on it.

Did Ganesha move eventually? Did he begin the race? Well, yes he did. He moved, not to dash around the world, but only to circle his parents. His parents were surprised.

Why was Ganesha still here? How would he cross continents, mountains, rivers and lakes if he did not leave?

Ganesha just kept circling his parents without a care in the world. His parents stared at him, looking very confused.

In a while, Ganesha came up to his parents and said,

"Divine parents, I have circled the world so many times. Give me the fruit and declare me first."

"Ganesha, we cannot do that. You did not circle the world with its seas, mountains and continents. You just hovered and circled around us," admonished his parents gently.

"But I have circled the world and come first father," Ganesha insisted.

"What?" uttered the two puzzled parents.

Ganesha bowed in front of Shiva and Parvati and said solemnly,

"You two, are the world! My heavenly parents represent the entire manifested universe."

Hearing this, Shiva and Parvati broke into a cheer and proudly acknowledged that for a boy so young, Ganesha was really very wise. When Kartekeya returned, he was told of what Ganesha had said. He too had to agree that Ganesha had shown very mature wisdom. Thus, Ganesha was declared the elder of the two and given the precious fruit.

Shiva, the Fisherman

One day, sitting at their abode, Mount Kailash, Lord Shiva was extremely irritated with his wife Parvati. There was no great reason for it; except that she was taking very long in absorbing her lessons from the Vedas.

You are no better than a fisherwoman

Eventually, Lord Shiva lost his temper and said, "Go and take birth as a fisherwoman. Your intelligence is no better than her."

POOOOOF!

Parvati disappeared!

Whatever Shiva wished for was bound to happen.

Staring into the empty space, where Parvati had just been sitting, Shiva groaned,

"How stupid of me?"

As days went by, Shiva missed Parvati very much. That made him gloomy and quiet. Nandi, his attendant, was quite disturbed at seeing Shiva in that condition.

Nandi mused, "My master will not be happy until his beloved comes back to Mount Kailash."

Meanwhile, other interesting events were unfolding on earth. Parvati had taken a new incarnation. She was born as a baby girl. Her manifestation took place under a tree. The headman of a fishermen community, incidentally, was passing by.

You are my daughter from now

Noticing the apparently abandoned baby, lying under the tree, he picked her up and took her home.

"You are my daughter now. I shall call you Parvati," said the fisherman, glancing indulgently at the gurgling baby.

Parvati grew up learning the ropes of catching fish. Her adopted father expertly tutored her on implements, weather and boats. Soon, she began to accompany her father on his fishing trips. She could row the boats faster than anyone else. Parvati had grown into a beautiful young woman. Apart from being good looking, she had a gentle and kind nature too.

Way above, from the environs of Mount Kailash, Nandi and Shiva observed all these happenings. Every time Shiva would see Parvati on earth, his heart would sink.

Pangs of despair and anger troubled him, "How could I send Parvati off like that?" Shiva questioned himself again and again.

"Lord, what is stopping you from going to earth and reclaiming Goddess Parvati?" asked Nandi.

"I cannot do that, Nandi. She is destined to marry a fisherman, who wins her hand in marriage," Lord Shiva shook his head and explained.

Nandi thoughtfully pondered over this statement. Obviously, he had a plan in mind.

The next morning, Nandi went to the seashore. Reciting *mantras,* he took the form of a large whale. Slipping into the seas, he swam to the exact location where Parvati's father's community fished. Reaching the area, Nandi then began to trouble the fishermen fishing there. He would bump into their boats, scare the fish, tear the nets or even chase boats out of the surrounding areas.

"We cannot fish in the sea anymore. A huge whale has taken up residence in those waters. It upturns our boats and tears off our nets. We cannot risk our lives this way," complained the fishermen.

If the fishermen decided to go on a strike, it would mean big trouble. Fishing was the only means of earning for this community. The headman quickly announced, "Listen, we must catch this menace. In fact, whoever can catch the whale, will get my daughter's hand in marriage."

Many single young fishermen rode into the seas with a bid to catch the whale and win Parvati. But they were all unsuccessful. It seemed the whale could never be caught. Parvati's father began to pray to Lord Shiva,

"We need your help, Lord. This menace is attacking our daily income. We will starve if nothing is done about it. Dear Lord, show us a way out of this problem," he prayed intensely.

Parvati joined him in his prayers too. As soon as Parvati began to chant Lord Shiva's name, Shiva heard her.

Immediately, Shiva changed into a handsome fisherman. Presenting himself to her father, the disguised Shiva offered, "I want to have a try at catching the whale."

Evidently impressed by the strapping young man's personality, the headman gave permission. The young fisherman rode the seas.

Catching the whale was no problem. Nandi, you see, had been waiting for this to happen all along! Once netted, Nandi wagged his whale tail gleefully.

Of course, Parvati married the handsome fisherman, who was actually Shiva. The trio of Shiva, Parvati and Nandi (back to his actual form) returned to Mount Kailash, once again.

When Krishna Lifted Mount Goverdhan

Young Krishna was disturbed by Lord Indra's behaviour.

"Lord Indra, the chief administrator of the heavens, is getting quite arrogant," Krishna mused now and then.

With this thought in mind, Krishna asked the people of Brajdham to stop worshipping Indra.

Now you will suffer

Krishna was so well respected that everyone automatically listened to him. Finding his devotees deserting him because Krishna told them to do so, Indra was inflamed.

In angry revenge, he summoned the blackest of rain clouds and ordered them to rain in a deluge over Brajdham. This order was promptly executed. Brajdham was under attack. Not by weapons but through rains accompanied by storms, lightening and thunder. The unending heavy rains grew into a natural calamity. The people of Brajdham were now battling a flood. Distressed, they begged Krishna to tell them what to do.

Krishna did not let them down. In front of many astonished eyes, he lifted the *Govardhan Parvat*, the largest mountain in the vicinity, in one heave.

Holding the mountain high, on his little finger, he instructed everyone to take cover under it, as he held it up. The entire village found safe haven under the mountain Krishna held.

Watching from the skies, Indra was dumbfounded. He continued to send storms and rains to Brajdham. Krishna was unaffected. He stood holding the mountain resolutely and unwaveringly. The mountain provided excellent cover for every one. The rains did not bother the people now, since they felt safe and did not care about Indra's manoeuvering any more. Soon, Lord Indra himself realized why Krishna had stopped people from praying to him.

"Hmmm, yes, I do think I was becoming arrogant. Sigh! Krishna was right in pointing this out. Gods have no right to be arrogant," Indra agreed with himself. Having understood Krishna's point, Indra instantly stopped the rains.

When the storms and rains were over, Lord Krishna asked the people to go back to their homes. Then he returned Govardhan Parvat to its original position.

The Magic Potion

One of the most famous kingdoms of ancient India was that of the *Kurus*. They had their capital at *Hastinapur* on the banks of the river *Ganga*. When Pandu, the king of Hastinapur died, his eldest son was very young. So, his elder brother Dhritrashtra, who was blind by birth, became the king. Dhritrashtra had a hundred sons who were called the Kauravas. Duryodhana was the eldest of all.

Pandavas

He nurtured dreams of laying claim to the throne after his father.

Pandu had five sons who were called the Pandavas. Their mother was Kunti. The eldest of the Pandavas was Yudhishthira. The second was Bhima, followed by Arjun, while the twins Nakul and Sahdev were the youngest. Duryodhana hated the Pandavas as he knew that Yudhishthira, being the eldest amongst them, was the rightful heir to the throne. Even though the Pandavas were affable boys, they could not help being affected by the apparent dislike shown by their Kaurava cousins.

Kauravas

Bitter rivalry began to strain the relationship between the brothers. Though the Kauravas hated all the Pandavas, they hated Bhima the most. Bhima was blessed with superhuman strength and was a prankster too. And often, the Kauravas were the victims of his pranks. He would shake them down from the trees when they were picking fruit; laughing hysterically as they came tumbling down. And if they tried to get rough with him, he would shake them off like little rats.

"We will get rid of him, once and for all," said Duryodhana viciously. "Without him, the Pandavas are nothing."

The Kauravas made a wicked plan. They invited the Pandavas to a picnic. The Pandavas were surprised by this sudden friendliness, but being good-natured boys, they accepted the invitation. Duryodhana specially told his cooks to prepare all of Bhima's favourite dishes.

Duryodhana, much to Bhima's astonishment, served him with his own hands, filling his plate up with meats and vegetables.

Unsuspectingly, Bhima ate all that he could and when he was done; he got up and walked down to the sandy shore. Suddenly, he felt a strange buzz in his head and his

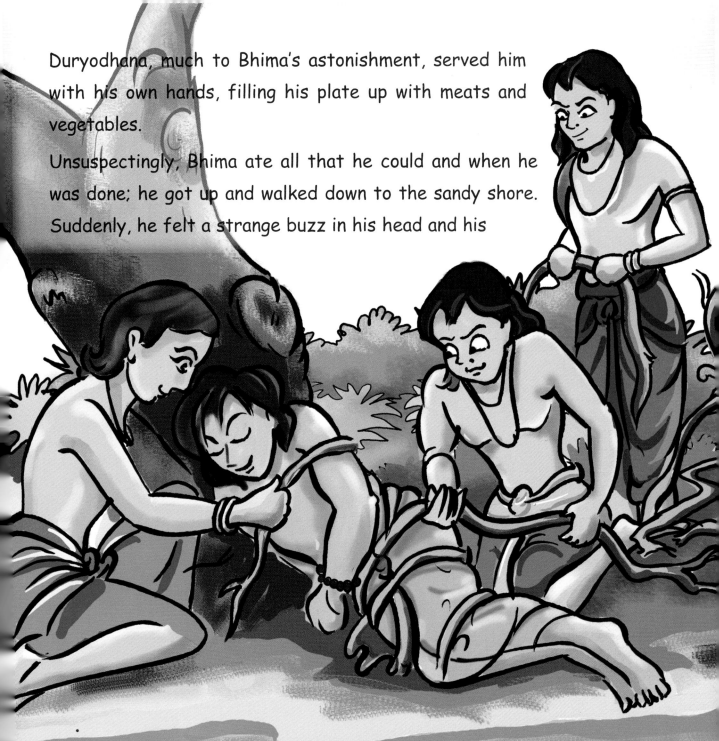

limbs felt heavy and sluggish. The next moment, he collapsed on the ground. Seeing this, the Kauravas hiding behind him, emerged on the scene.

"Quick! Cut some thick, strong vines," Duryodhana said to his brothers.

"Tie him up tightly," said one of the Kauravas.

"The poison is doing its work, but I'm taking no chances. Let's throw him into the river. With him dead, the Pandavas won't ever be able to lay claim to the throne," said Duryodhana.

The Kauravas bound Bhima's feet and arms with tough vines and threw him into the river.

The boy sank to the bottom and landed in a pit of *Nagas* or snakes. The *Nagas* looked at the strange creature in their midst and hissing with anger, they sank their fangs into his body. The poison flowed into Bhima's veins mixing with the poison already present. This proved to be an antidote. One poison destroyed the other effectively!

Instantly cured, Bhima opened his eyes. Flexing his powerful muscles, he broke his fetters. The snakes tried to attack him again, but he grabbed them and tore them into pieces. When news of this reached the great Serpent King, Vasuki, he said, "I must see this lad who can make my serpents quiver with fear. Take me to him." The king and his councillors found Bhima ringed by dead *Nagas*.

Bhima looked up and stared unafraid at the great Serpent king.

Vasuki liked the courage that Bhima displayed and said,

"You have shown great courage, my boy. I will give you a priceless gift as your reward." The *Nagas* led Bhima into a chamber where a number of small jars were kept.

"These jars contain *Rasakunda*, the elixir of strength," said Vasuki proudly. "Drink as much as you can. Each jar contains the strength of a thousand elephants."

Bhima opened one jar and downed it. Then he picked up a second and a third. The *Nagas* looked at him with dawning respect. Nobody had drunk more than two before. Bhima emptied eight jars and this was truly a magnificent feat.

"Now you must sleep," the Serpent king said, "each jar takes one day to digest. I am afraid you will be asleep for a while. When you wake up, you can go home."

They escorted Bhima to a chamber with a bed and Bhima fell into a deep, dreamless sleep. While in Hastinapur, Bhima's absence was a cause of worry for the Pandavas and their mother Kunti. Kunti quietly sent out search parties to look for Bhima, but there was no news. The Pandavas noticed their cousins' gloating faces but were helpless without proof, so they pretended they didn't know that the Kauravas were responsible.

Seven days passed, Kunti and the Pandavas were now sure that Bhima was dead. Far away from prying eyes, they wept into their pillows. The next morning, there was a shout in the hallway and Bhima burst into the room, eyes shining with excitement.

His brothers leapt up, laughing, hugging and bombarding him with questions.

"O! What an adventure," said Bhima, his eyes dancing. Then Bhima narrated the whole story to his mother and brothers.

"I killed a lot of snakes," Bhima said laughingly. His mother and brothers did not find the thought of his being poisoned a laughing matter. But they decided to put it behind in the best interests of the family. The Kauravas soon learnt that Bhima was back, stronger than ever.

"He got lucky this time," Duryodhana said, "but there is always a next time."

The enmity between the Kauravas and the Pandavas would result in a war, which would be named the *Mahabharata*.

The Greatest Archer

Drona was a stern teacher. One morning, Drona asked the Kuru princes to assemble in the target ranges with their bows and arrows.

"Do you see the artificial bird in the tree?" Drona asked his students.

"Yes sir," the students said in unison.

"The aim is to hit the bird's eye," Drona said, "you will each get one chance. Yudhishthira, you first."

The eldest Pandava positioned himself and raising his bow, drew back the bowstring. But before he could release the arrow, Drona said,

"Wait! What do you see?"

"I see the tree, the leaves, the sky, the bird..."

"Back to your place," Drona interrupted angrily, "you have learnt nothing."

One by one, the princes were asked to aim at the bird and each was asked the same question. All the answers were like Yudhishthira's and with every answer, Drona became angrier.

Arjun was the last to be called. As Arjun drew back the bowstring, he was asked scornfully,

"What do you see?"

"The bird's eye,"

Arjun said, eye on the target.

"What else? The trees, the sky, me?"

Drona asked sarcastically.

"No sir, just the bird's eye,"

Arjun replied.

"Come on now, Arjun! You can surely see the bird."

"No sir," Arjun replied confidently, "just the eye of the bird."

The angry scowl disappeared and a faint smile curved Drona's lips.

"Release the arrow," he commanded. The arrow flew with great speed and accuracy and hit the bird's eye. The bird fell to the ground with a thud. Drona turned and said to the others,

"You all have learnt nothing. Had this been war, none of you would have hit the mark. You would have all been dead. Except for Arjun," Drona said, looking fondly at Arjun,

"only he has learnt the most important lesson in archery: *the target is all that the eye must see.* Mark my words, Arjun will become the greatest archer the world has ever seen," concluded Drona.

Eklavya's Guru Dakshina

Once, the Kuru princes were hunting, when suddenly, they chanced upon a *Nishada* (forest dweller) youth being attacked by a dog. The *Nishada* was practicing archery, before the dog assaulted him. Barking furiously, the dog lunged towards the Nishada. Before the dog could close its mouth in a bite; the Nishada drew back his bowstring and quickly shot seven arrows into the gaping jaws, keeping them wrenched apart.

The dog now couldn't shut its mouth. Yelping in pain, it ran away.

The princes were stunned. They had just witnessed the most brilliant piece of archery! Unfazed, the Nishada continued aiming arrows and hitting bull's eye expertly on the target he had been practicing on.

The princes watched him with silent admiration.

Arjun was watching too. But his heart was filled with jealousy. Arjun till now was hailed as the best archer. Evidently, it seemed he had a rival, who seemed to be way better than him.

With some effort, Arjun finally spoke.

"Who are you?" choked Arjun jealously.

"I am Eklavya, prince of the Nishadas," answered the young boy.

"Who is your guru?" asked Arjun again, unable to hide his feelings.

"My guru is Dronacharya," replied Eklavya.

On hearing this, Arjun turned about and raced back to Gurukul.

Reaching, he rushed into Drona's chamber. Drona noticed Arjun's expression and asked, "Arjun, is something bothering you?"

"You told me that I would be the world's greatest archer," Arjun burst

out, "yet today I saw a Nishada in the forest, who makes me look like an amateur; and he says you are his guru. Tell me how can that be?"

"Take me to this boy," Drona said without emotion. Arjun led Drona towards the forest.

When Eklavya saw Drona, he dropped his bow and humbly touched his feet. The clear eyes looked at him with unconditional love and devotion.

But Drona's eyes revealed nothing as he looked down at the boy. At the far end, Drona saw a crude clay image of himself garlanded with wild flowers.

"How am I your guru?" Drona asked abruptly.

"Many years ago, I came to you and asked you to be my guru," Eklavya said, "but you refused because I am a poor forest dweller," he added sadly. "Yet, I never sought another guru as my heart had chosen you and would not choose again. So, I returned to the forest and made this clay statue of you. Every day, before I begin my practice, I pray to you and seek your guidance."

Drona listened to him with a cold face. He looked at Arjun who was quiet.

Then he turned to Eklavya, "If I am your guru, you owe me my fee or *guru dakshina*."

"Anything," Eklavya said excitedly, "there is nothing I will not give my guru."

Give me my guru dakshina

"If that is the case, then give me the thumb of your right hand," Drona said emotionlessly.

The other princes were horrified on hearing this.

What was an archer without his thumb?

But Eklavya, without the slightest hesitation, drew out his hunting knife and cut off his thumb. Then, he held out the bleeding limb to Drona who took it quickly and walked away swiftly. The princes followed him in shocked silence. Only Arjun showed no sign of sorrow. Eklavya picked up his bow and shot an arrow. The arrow flew with amazing speed and accuracy. The skill was there but the magic that had marked it was gone forever.

The Bet

One day, Arjun was challenged by a monkey to build a bridge of arrows. "I will step on to the bridge of arrows made by you and break it," proclaimed the monkey proudly.

"That is not possible," Arjun exclaimed in disbelief. Now every one knew that if Arjun made a bridge of arrows, he would a make a strong, unbreakable one. He was the king archer of those times and hated to be challenged.

The monkey, however, continued to confront Arjun.

"Well, Arjun, you seem very sure of your prowess. However, I would like to lay a bet. My bet says that if I cannot break your bridge of arrows, I will be declared your lifetime slave."

Arjun was so charged on hearing this bet that he said, "Yes and if I lose, I will kill myself in a fire pyre."

"So be it," the monkey seriously nodded.

With the terms of the bet settled, Arjun decided to build the bridge of arrows across the sea. Standing by the shore, Arjun sent out a barrage of arrows. With quick silver skill, he soon built a strong bridge.

"Walk across my unbreakable bridge now, dear monkey," Arjun said flourishing a hand towards the entry of the bridge. With a confident stride, the monkey stepped on to the bridge.

WWWAAARRRRPPPPP! The bridge split into two; breaking almost instantly.

Arjun was very impressed.

"I lose the challenge and accept the punishment," he solemnly said. The monkey pranced here and there gleefully.

Arjun lit a pyre. As soon as he was going to step into it, he was interrupted. Who interrupted him? A little boy. This boy materialized out of thin air. Coming closer, he asked Arjun why he was stepping into the pyre. When Arjun told him, the boy begged him to build one more bridge.

"Please continue the challenge. Let us see if this dear monkey can break the second bridge too."

Why is it not breaking?

Seeing the young boy pleading, Arjun and the monkey decided to humour him. In a few moments, Arjun swiftly constructed another bridge of arrows.

Once again, the monkey stepped on it. But this time, the bridge did not break. The monkey tried his level best but the bridge stood firm and strong.

Now, let us tell you a secret. The monkey was actually Hanuman, the monkey God. Hanuman was used to having his strength put to test. He collected his powers within himself and in desperation tried to break the bridge. He grew to an enormous size and jumped.

But the bridge did not break even then. Hanuman was frustrated.

"What's wrong with me ? I feel all my strength is ebbing out of me," he muttered helplessly.

Meanwhile, Arjun turned to the little boy and fell to his knees,

"I know you are not an ordinary child."

By now, Hanuman too had reached the same conclusion.

He left the bridge and knelt besides Arjun. The boy surveyed the two, then smiled. A huge mass of air rose before them. The boy was hidden completely. When the cloud cleared, Lord Vishnu stood before them.

"Arjun, you forgot to be humble. That is why Hanuman broke your bridge at first. As for you Hanuman, you became boastful. As a punishment, you will have to be on Arjun's flag pole all the time."

"Your wish is our command," Arjun and Hanuman bowed and agreed immediately.

Bhima & Jarasandha

Yudhishthira, the eldest of the Pandava brothers, expressed a desire to be declared emperor of the entire realm. However, he needed to perform the *Rajasuya yagna* for that. He also needed complete control of all the kingdoms, unopposed by anyone, to his credit, before he could begin the yagna.

This wish of Yudhishthira was discussed amongst the Pandavas. When these discussions were taking place, Krishna was present too. Krishna brought to everyone's attention the fact that the tyrant King Jarasandha of Magadh, would fiercely oppose this claim of Yudhishthira.

Jarasandha was a dictator and created a terrible issue. He had oppressed and captured eighty-six princes from the surrounding kingdoms. With Yudhishthira planning the Rajasuya yagna, an opportunity had presented itself to address this issue. Yudhishthira, however, was a peace loving king. He hated to create unpleasantness with his neighbours.

His reluctance was brushed away by Arjun and Bhima.

Jarasandha will oppose your claim

They wanted to fight this evil king and rescue the captured princes. Moreover, they wanted to dethrone Jarasandha so Yudishthira could proceed with the Rajasuya yagna.

It was not easy to depose Jarasandha because he had a special gift. The legend goes that when Jarasandha was born, he had only half a body. His worried parents approached a medicine woman, who by her magical cures, made Jarasandha's body whole again. Jarasandha now had two separate parts of his body flimsily joined together. It was said that even if the separate parts of his body broke into two, he could rejoin his body within minutes and rise again. Through the medicine woman, he was also given super natural strength and a boon that no weapon could kill him. That is why Jarasandha became so arrogant. He went berserk, claiming power and vanquishing kingdoms.

You don't look
like brahmins

After much planning, Bhima, Arjun and Krishna, decided to meet Jarasandha and challenge him.

They disguised themselves as wandering brahmins and reached the city of Magadh. Meanwhile, Jarasandha had invited brahmins from all over the empire to visit his court. He wanted to task them with the job of doing special prayers for his welfare. The three did not miss this opening of entering Jarasandha's court. With scores of other brahmins invited to perform the special prayers, the three also arrived at the royal court.

When the king granted the brahmins an audience, his sharp gaze narrowed down to the three. Noticing their well built bodies and scarred hands, Jarasandha commented, "You are dressed like brahmins but do not seem to be brahmins."

When Jarasandha looked closer, he recognized Bhima, Arjun and Krishna. As soon as they knew their disguise was exposed, Krishna without waiting, announced, "Yes, we are not brahmins. You have recognized us correctly. Jarasandha, we have come to challenge you to a duel."

Highly amused, Jarasandha rubbed his hands and said discerningly, "I will only duel with the strongest of the three. I choose to fight Bhima, who is just about equal to me in strength."

Having said that, an arena was prepared and Bhima and Jarasandha began to wrestle. The fight was equally placed. It went on for days. Each day brought fresher challenges for the opponents. However, there came a moment when Jarasandha slipped and grabbing the chance, Bhima rolled him over and effortlessly snapped his body into two halves. Flinging the parts away, Bhima raised his hands in victory and ran towards Arjun and Krishna.

Oh dear, right behind him, the two parts of Jarasandha's body crept towards each other and joined up! Instantly, Jarasandha stood again. The duel continued. Days flew by, but the wrestling continued. Jarasandha seemed to have more strength then ever. Bhima was getting tired. One day, his eyes wandered to Krishna, even though his limbs were locked in a deadly embrace with Jarasandha. Krishna saw him, nodded, then did a strange thing.

He bent and picked up a twig. Raising the twig, he broke it into two. Then, he crossed his hands over his chest and threw the two pieces over his shoulders.

This way, the piece in his right hand flew to the left and the twig in his left hand, flew to the right!

Bhima immediately understood the tactic. In a rush of strength, he battered Jarasandha and gained an advantage. With a roar, he raised Jarasandha's body. Placing it over his knee, once again, snapped it into two halves; crossed his hands and flung the halves over his shoulders. Now, both the parts were opposite to each other. The more they crawled to join up, the more they moved further away.

That is how Jarasandha was killed. The captured princes were freed and Yudhishthira prepared for doing the Rajasuya yagna peacefully.

The Death of Abhimanyu

The saga of Mahabharata is full of stories that speak continuously of valour and sad sacrifices. However, one tale that touches the heart is the story of the death of Abhimanyu, Arjun's sixteen year old son.

The story begins at the point when the battles were raging and the Kaurava generals saw victory slipping from their hands rapidly.

In desperation, Drona now took command of the Kaurava armies. He arranged the soldiers in the formation of a *chakravyuha*. What is a *chakravyuha*? This was a confusing circular military formation. Only a few people knew the key of escaping this chakravyuha.

Arjun, of course, was the only Pandava who knew how to breach the chakravyuha. Sadly, he was away at another front, fighting.

The older Pandava brothers, Yudhishthira and Bhima, found breaking into the chakravyuha next to impossible. But breaching the difficult formation was very important, if the Pandavas did not want to lose the war. Thus, they needed to come up with another strategy. Intense debates and plans were thrashed in order to unravel the chakravyuha.

But no solution could be reached. Finally, with a grim face, Yudhishthira announced, "Ask Abhimanyu to come here."

When Abhimanyu arrived, after the usual salutations, Yudhishthira explained the situation saying, "Drona has created a chakravyuha formation with his troops. As we are all aware, only four men know the key to breaching this complex stationing of soldiers. Of the four, Krishna, your father Arjun and Krishna's son are not here. That leaves you. I need you to infiltrate that base and smash through into the chakravyuha.

Now there was a problem. Abhimanyu knew how to infiltrate the chakravyuha, but did not know how to get out.

The assembled group realized that if Abhimanyu entered the chakravyuha and could not get out, it would mean his death.

"We will bring up the rear-guard. They will closely follow you as you enter," the Pandava generals suggested.

As soon as Abhimanyu was given the go-ahead, the brave young prince, with a lusty war cry, tore through the enemy ranks, sending the most seasoned of Kaurava warriors, yelping for cover. Cleaving a swathe with his brandishing sword, Abhimanyu broke the chakravyuha and reached its center effortlessly.

The Kauravas were quick to react. In ferocious retaliation, they hacked back the rear guard and managed to isolate Abhimanyu in the center of the chakravyuha.

Sealed from all sides Abhimanyu found himself in the middle of his enemies.

The Kauravas wasted no time in assaulting him. Undeterred, Abhimanyu fought back expertly. He kept the Kauravas at bay in fierce combat. "Surround him. Close in, then kill him," Duryodhan snarled, not liking the way the battle was moving.

Encircling Abhimanyu, the Kauravas pierced him with showers of arrows. Badly struck, yet his determination unaffected, Abhimanyu competed so courageously that there was panic in the Kaurava camp.

"What do we do?" the Kaurava generals cried to Drona, "He is slaughtering us!"

Though Drona was thoroughly impressed with Abhimanyu's bravery, he, due to unfortunate circumstances, belonged to the Kaurava side. In a cold voice, Drona suggested, "Disarm him completely and cut off his armour."

This plan was immediately put into action. Abhimanyu was enclosed by hefty warriors. They rampaged in first killing Abhimanyu's charioteer. With vile intent, they slowly gained advantage.

Young Abhimanyu fought well. But he was outnumbered.

Even though, he was completely disarmed, he picked up the wheel of his chariot and continued to fight. But he could not deflect the final, fatal blow rendered on him.

As Abhimanyu's breath stilled, overhead from the skies, voices protested, *"So many against one; this was an unfair battle."*

More voices rose, "Hail brave Abhimanyu, shame on the Kauravas," protests rang through the skies.

This sad tale would be told and retold. There would always be regret at Abhimanyu's brutal death. But no one would forget Abhimanyu's fight for survival. This way Abhimanyu's name would be written in the annals of the epic; he would be called one of the bravest soldiers there ever was.

The Day Vishnu became an Arrow

"Ha! ha! ha!" The three demon brothers, menancingly hovered over the heavens. Now these demons were not airbourne in their wind chariots, they were floating in three separate flying cities! But how was that possible? Flying cities? Yes, these demons were the sons of the mighty demon, Taraka. Though Taraka was dead, his sons were becoming a threat. Long ago, by the austerity of their prayers, they obtained a boon from Lord Brahma. Overwhelmed by their prayers, Brahma granted them these cities.

"One gold, one silver and one iron city for each of you. Each city will have the capacity to fly too," blessed Brahma. Not only that, Brahma was so pleased that he enhanced the boon saying,

"I grant you such might that your cities cannot be destroyed, unless they are struck by a single arrow, shot by a divine archer and only when the cities are in one single line."

The three demon brothers, instead of responsibly handling this boon, misused its power. Meandering in a threat, never allowing their cities to be in one line, they took control of the three worlds. Now, challenging three flying cities, was just about too much for the Gods to handle. Frustrated beyond words, they formed an assembly and approached Shiva.

"Help us, dear Lord! Life in the heavens and earth is miserable because of these buoyant demon brothers with flying cities."

Shiva nodded, "I will help."

Thus, it was declared that Shiva was the chosen archer. Meru was the shaft of his bow and Sheshnaga (Shiva's snake) his bowstring. The earth was his chariot, the sun and the moon were its wheels. Brahma was the charioteer and the four books of the Veda were his horses. Shiva waited for the cities to align in a single line.

But the cities kept flying in different directions; such was their will to survive. Alas, Shiva gave up. Gloom cast an unhappy shadow all around.

"Listen, don't get disheartened. I have a plan," offered Vishnu. Vishnu carried out his plan. He took the form of a monk and visited the three cities. As a monk, Vishnu started to give lectures on existence. He slowly gained fame as a wise and knowledgable monk. The three demon brothers too heard of him. Right from the first lecture they heard, the brothers were mesmerized by the monk. They intently began to attend the wandering monk's sessions. Vishnu taught the demons the doctrine of releasing their soul from worldly goods. Eventually, the demons lost all interest in worldly life. They did not bother to fly their cities in different directions.

This was the moment the Devas were waiting for. One day, when the demons were lulled into a deep meditation by Vishnu and they did not notice that the three cites lay in one single line, the Gods struck!

Taking advantage of the situation, Shiva drew his great bow. Do you know who was the arrow? None other than Vishnu himself! Yes, Vishnu served as Shiva's arrow. Shiva twanged his bow and Vishnu hit all three cities, destroying them in an instant. As the victorious Gods cheered, Shiva smeared his body with the ash of the cities on his body, in three horizontal lines.

Indra's Palace

"**B**uild me a magnificent palace dear architect of *Swarga loka*," Lord Indra, king of the heavens, smilingly asked Vishwakarma, the celestial architect.

Vishwakarma immediately built a magnificent palace. Oh dear, Indra was not satisfied at all.

"I am Lord Indra, for me, this palace is not good enough."

Poor Vishwakarma carried on with his assignment. He made many more palaces, each more magnificent than the previous, but Indra was not satisfied.

"This is just not good enough for me," remarked Indra.

Lord Vishnu, the Great God, was observing this.

"Indra's ego needs to be humbled," he decided. Disguising himself as a young boy, Lord Vishnu approached Indra and said,

"May I see your palace?"

"Yes, but why do you want to see my palace?" questioned Indra.

"So I can compare it with the palaces of the other Indras," replied the boy.

"Other Indras? There is only one Indra, that is me," Indra uttered in a perplexed tone.

"Oh! Did you think that you were the only Indra that shall exist in this sea of time? No, there are and will be many Indras before and after you. Each Indra will ask Vishwakarma to make grand palaces but will that make them grand actually? Or will it just fulfill the need of a false ego?"

Indra immediately understood what the boy was trying to tell him. He also realized that the boy in front of him was not an ordinary boy, but someone divine.

Lord Vishnu revealed himself and Indra apologized to him for having false pride and vanity.

Children Books By

Great Stories for Children *Series*

Size: 8" x 11" – Pages: 48 – Hardbound All Colour

Great Stories For Children
(Red Book)

Great Stories For Children
(Green Book)

Great Stories For Children
(Purple Book)

Great Stories For Children
(Yellow Book)

Great Stories For Children
(Black Book)

Great Stories For Children
(White Book)

Great Stories For Children
(Orange Book)

Great Stories For Children
(Brown Book)

Each book is a collection of stories from Indian folklore and myths. Every story is beautifully illustrated and accompanied with appropriate morals to impart wisdom to children. This is a series of 10 books - Red, Yellow, Green, Blue, Pink, Purple, Brown, Orange, Black and White. Each colour book has a different set of stories.

Great Stories For Children
(Blue Book)

Great Stories For Children
(Pink Book)

Children Books By

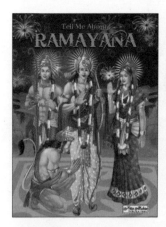

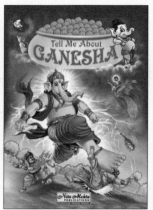

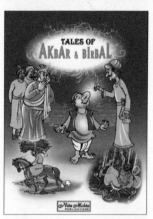

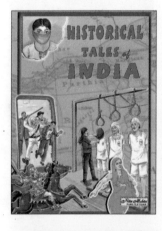

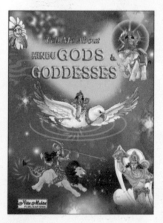

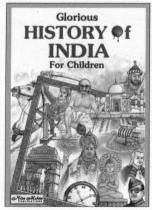